NATHAN HALE

PATRIOT SPY

by SHANNON ZEMLICKA
illustrations by CRAIG ORBACK

Carolrhoda Books, Inc./Minneapolis

All dialogue in this book is taken from written records related to Nathan Hale's life, as collected in *Documentary Life of Nathan Hale*, edited by George Dudley Seymour (New Haven, CT: privately printed, 1942).

The illustrator would like to thank the models who were used for the oil paintings, most especially Eric Janzen as Nathan Hale, and Bryan Woolley, Lanny O'Cain, Megan O'Cain, and Matthew O'Cain as assorted characters.

The photograph on page 46 appears with permission from Thomas P. Benincas, Jr.

This book is available in two editions:
Library binding by Carolrhoda Books, Inc., a division of Lerner Publishing Group
Soft cover by First Avenue Editions, an imprint of Lerner Publishing Group
241 First Avenue North
Minneapolis, Minnesota 55401 U.S.A.

Website address: www.lernerbooks.com

Library of Congress Cataloging-in-Publication Data

Zemlicka, Shannon.
    Nathan Hale : patriot spy / by Shannon Zemlicka ; illustrations by Craig Orback.
        p.   cm. — (On my own biography)
    Summary: Recounts the life of Revolutionary War hero Nathan Hale, whose decision to become a spy for General George Washington cost him his life.
    ISBN: 0–87614–597–7 (lib. bdg. : alk. paper)
    ISBN: 0–87614–905–0 (pbk. : alk. paper)
    1. Hale, Nathan, 1755–1776—Juvenile literature. 2. United States—History—Revolution, 1775–1783—Secret service—Juvenile literature. 3. Spies—United States—Biography—Juvenile literature. 4. Soldiers—United States—Biography—Juvenile literature. [1. Hale, Nathan, 1755–1776. 2. Spies. 3. United States—History—Revolution, 1775–1783—Secret service.] I. Title. II. Series.
E280.H2 Z46 2002
973.3'85'092—dc21   2001004820

Manufactured in the United States of America
1 2 3 4 5 6 – JR – 07 06 05 04 03 02

For Kyle, a great fan of spy stories — S. Z.

*For my parents, Gary and Eileen, for their support,
and for grandma Ethel Schneider for her support
and inspiration— C. S. O.*

A Young American
Connecticut, 1769

Nathan Hale sat tall and proud on his horse.
He was 14 years old,
almost a man.
This was an important day.
He and his brother Enoch
were on their way to Yale College.

Nathan was lucky.

He came from a family that prized learning
and could afford to pay for it.

Nathan's parents owned a large farm.

They had 12 children to feed.

But they had found the money to send
Nathan and Enoch to college.

Nathan loved going to Yale.

He didn't mind his classes or homework.

He read for hours about

heroes and warriors of long ago.

He even joined a secret club

to talk about books.

Nathan also spent time outdoors.

He could run fast and jump far.

He could beat almost anyone
at wrestling.

With his kind smile,

Nathan made friends easily.

Just about everyone who knew
him liked him.

While Nathan grew and changed,
his world was changing, too.
America was not a free country.
It was a group of colonies,
settlements ruled by another country.
Many Americans were unhappy
with their ruler, King George III of Britain.

He gave the colonies little freedom.
Americans had to pay high taxes.
They had no voice
in the British government.
People were getting angrier and angrier.

When Nathan finished college in 1773,
he became a teacher.
He liked helping children learn.
And his students liked their new teacher.
In New London, Connecticut,
he even held classes for girls.

Most people believed that girls
didn't need to go to school.
Nathan did not agree.
He invited the girls of New London
to come to school early in the morning,
before their brothers did.

Nathan made his students follow his rules,

but he could be fun, too.

He amazed the children by doing stunts.

He could leap from inside one barrel

all the way into another.

And he could put his hand on a tall fence

and vault right over it.

Nathan thought he might like to be

a teacher for the rest of his life.

But everything changed in April of 1775.

In Massachusetts, British troops fired

on a group of farmers.

The farmers were patriots,

people who believed America should be free.

Suddenly America was going to war.

Nathan joined his neighbors
at a town meeting.
Some of them were scared.
Britain had a powerful army
and plenty of money for weapons.
The Americans had few soldiers
and little money.
How could they hope to win?

Maybe America should just make peace.

Nathan didn't think so.

It was wrong for a faraway king
to rule the colonies so harshly.

Win or lose, America had to fight.

Nathan stood up to speak.

In a loud, ringing voice, he cried,
"Let us march immediately!"

Nathan wanted to join
the patriot army right away.
But he had promised
to teach school until July.
Then he received an exciting letter.
It was an offer to join the army
as an officer!
He would be in charge of
his own group of soldiers.
Nathan gave up his teaching job
two weeks early.
He took each student by the hand
and said good-bye.
He was on his way to serve in the fight
for American freedom.

A Bold Leader
Boston, November 1775

"March!" shouted Nathan.
He and his men had been training
near Boston for weeks.
The city was full of British troops.
But no one was fighting.
General George Washington had
surrounded the city with his army.
He was waiting for the British
to give up and sail away.

Nathan didn't like waiting.
He didn't feel much like
the heroes he had read about in college.
Instead of doing brave deeds,
he and his men drilled and drilled.
In their free time,
they played checkers and soccer.
Nathan wished he could do more
to help America win the war.

Soon winter came.

The patriot soldiers had few warm clothes.

The fields grew muddy, then snowy.

The men were hungry.

They hated drilling in the cold.

Some got sick.

Nathan visited them in their tents
and prayed with them.
He tried to keep up everyone's spirits.
But all over George Washington's army,
men were giving up and going home.
To keep his soldiers,
Nathan gave them his own pay.

In January of 1776,

Nathan was made a captain.

He was put in charge of two lieutenants

and all their men.

That March, the British fled Boston.

General Washington thought

they might attack New York City next.

He sent many soldiers there,

including Nathan and his men.

From his new camp, Nathan saw

British ships anchored in the East River.

One was a small ship called a sloop.

It carried supplies and weapons.

The patriots needed weapons badly.

Nathan saw a chance

to do something important at last.

One night, Nathan led a few men
to the sloop in a rowboat.

They had to be careful.

A huge warship, the *Asia*, guarded the sloop.

Nathan and his men climbed onto the sloop.

They surprised the crew
and cut the sloop loose.

No one on the *Asia* spotted them.

Nathan sailed the sloop
straight to the patriots.

He and his men had captured
a whole ship full of supplies and weapons!
A few months after his daring adventure,
Nathan was given a place in the Rangers.
This new group of soldiers would carry out
special tasks for General Washington.
Perhaps Nathan Hale could make himself
useful again soon.

A Dangerous Task
Manhattan, New York, September 1776

One night, Colonel Thomas Knowlton
called together the four Ranger captains.
He had a request for them.

Things looked grim for the patriots.

British troops had beaten them badly

at Long Island in August.

General Washington needed help.

He had to know how many troops

the British had on Long Island.

Where were they?

When would they attack?

There was just one way to find out,

Colonel Knowlton said.

George Washington needed a spy.

Nathan could not offer to go.

He had been very sick.

He did not have the strength

for such a dangerous task.

The other Rangers looked at each other.

They looked up at the ceiling.

They looked down at their shoes.

They looked everywhere

except at Colonel Knowlton.

General Washington needed a spy?

But spying was dangerous!

Spying meant sneaking and lying.

It meant lurking and hiding.

If a man was caught spying,

the best he could expect was a quick death.

Besides, spying wasn't honorable.

Fighting on the battlefield was one thing.

But no honest officer would agree to be a spy.

No one volunteered that night.
But soon Colonel Knowlton called
his officers together again.
General Washington still needed a spy.
Would no one help him?
Nathan Hale was no longer sick.
He stepped forward
and looked the colonel in the eye.
He would do it, he said.
He would become
George Washington's spy.

Nathan began to make plans.

He told his friend William Hull

that he would wear a disguise.

Then he would sneak

into the British camps.

William was shocked.

How could Nathan do such a thing?

Spying was for liars and cheats.

No one would respect Nathan if he went.

Besides, Nathan wouldn't make a good spy.

He was much too honest.

The British would catch him and hang him.

Nathan must not go, William urged.

Nathan listened carefully to his friend.

"I wish to be useful," he explained.

He knew the job was dangerous.

But if spying would help his country,

it was honorable to him.

He shook William's hand

and promised to think things over.

It must have been hard
to go against a friend's advice.
It must have been hard to do something
that so many people thought was wrong.
But Nathan didn't change his mind.
George Washington needed him.
America needed him.
He would go to Long Island
as a patriot spy.

Patriot Spy

Long Island, New York, September 1776

Soon after his talk with William,
Nathan boarded a ship for Long Island.
He left behind his captain's uniform
and his gun.
He wore only the plain clothes
of a common teacher.

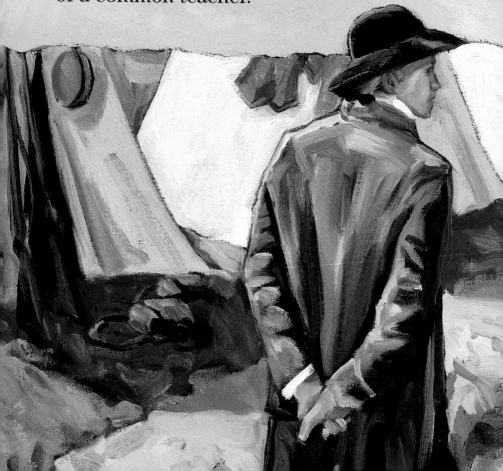

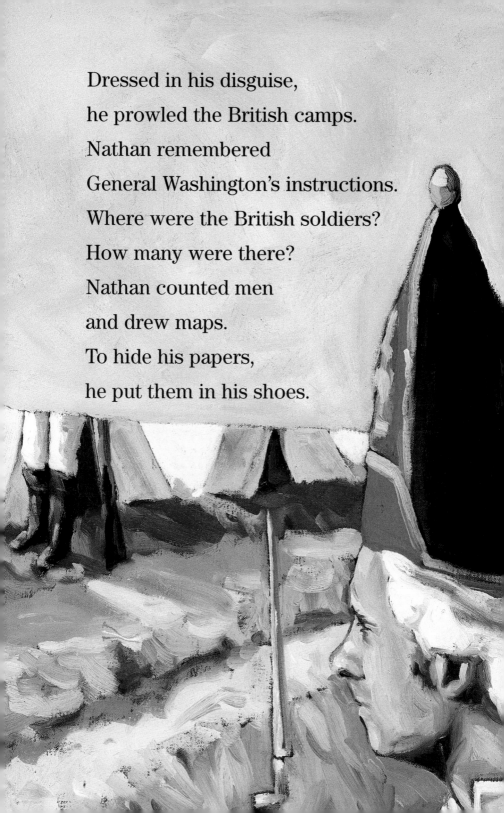

Dressed in his disguise,
he prowled the British camps.
Nathan remembered
General Washington's instructions.
Where were the British soldiers?
How many were there?
Nathan counted men
and drew maps.
To hide his papers,
he put them in his shoes.

After about nine days,

Nathan had learned all he could.

He started back toward the patriots' camp.

No one knows for sure

exactly what happened next.

Somehow, Nathan was captured
and made a prisoner of the British.
A soldier searched his shoes
and found his maps and notes.
He was brought to General William Howe.
Howe was the commander
of Britain's troops in America.

General Howe asked why Nathan

was wandering among his camps.

Nathan could have tried to lie.

But he was not a liar.

He told the truth.

He was a patriot officer

and a spy for General Washington.

General Howe was furious.

How dare this bold young man

spy on his soldiers?

He ordered his men to hang Nathan

the very next morning.

Nathan spent that night
locked in a greenhouse
near the general's headquarters.
A guard stood outside the door.
Nathan had no chance to escape.
He could only think about his country,
his family, and his God.
He could only try to prepare himself
for what would happen the next day.
The next morning, September 22,
Nathan asked his jailer for two favors.
Could a minister visit him?
And could he have a Bible to read?

The jailer said no.

A spy deserved nothing

but the hangman's rope.

Nathan was allowed to write to his brother

and to Colonel Knowlton.

But the jailer destroyed the letters later.

At last, Nathan was brought outside.

He knew that his life was about to end.

But he was calm.

There was just one thing that

he was sorry about, he said.

"I only regret that I have but one life

to lose for my country."

After Nathan spoke, British soldiers

put a rope around his neck

and hanged him.

The life of Nathan Hale,

patriot, soldier, and spy, had ended.

But the story of Nathan Hale,

American hero, had just begun.

This statue of Nathan Hale at Yale University in New Haven, Connecticut, stands outside the classroom where Nathan once studied.

Afterword

After Nathan was captured, some Americans said that he had been betrayed. Nathan's cousin Samuel Hale supported the British and was working for them on Long Island. Some people said that Samuel had recognized Nathan and turned him in. No one knows for certain whether the story is true.

Why do we remember Nathan Hale? He didn't succeed in his mission to give George Washington the information he needed. And he didn't inspire his fellow soldiers, since most of them never heard about what he did.

What makes Nathan Hale special is the kind of person he was. Like many brave people, he fought for America's freedom when no one could guess who would win the war. But for Nathan, the desire to be useful to his young country went farther. He was willing to give up the respect of the people he respected to answer George Washington's call. And he was willing to give up his own life.

Nathan didn't live to see his dream of American freedom come true. The Revolutionary War continued for seven more long years. By the war's end, the colonies had won the freedom to become states and form their own nation. The United States of America came into being thanks to the courage of people like Nathan Hale, a true American hero.

Important Dates

1755—Nathan Hale is born in Coventry, Connecticut, on June 6.

1769—Entered Yale College, which later became Yale University, in New Haven, Connecticut

1773—Argued in favor of education for girls; graduated from Yale; taught school in East Haddam, Connecticut

1774—Taught school in New London, Connecticut

April 1775—Spoke in favor of war at town meeting in New London

July 1775—Became a lieutenant in Seventh Connecticut Regiment

September 1775—Arrived in Boston with his soldiers

January 1776—Promoted to captain

April 1776—Arrived with soldiers in New York

May 1776—Stole British supply ship

September 1776—Joined Knowlton's Rangers; spied on British solidiers on Long Island; captured by the British; hanged September 22